Women Served There, Too
Enlisted Women in Vietnam
by
Amanda Oviatt

This work was originally written as a research paper for a graduate level course on Vietnam History.

References to copyrighted material are posted in the "works Cited" section of the text.

Published by Amanda Oviatt

Dedication:

To all the women who served before me, with me, and since my time in the service.

We've shown the world what it means to be a warrior.

Warning about Tet

In December of 1967, intelligence analyst Doris "Lucki" Allen discovered that the enemy forces were planning a major operation. This operation was going to include roughly 50,000 enemy forces. She was new to Vietnam, and thought all of the Viet Cong were dead, so she assumed these forces were Chinese. These soldiers were going to "clobber the bejezus out of us." While she did not know the actual date, she knew the approximate date for the attack, and typed up a report to deliver to Headquarters, MACV. The officers at MACV ignored her report. Allen thought, "If we don't do something about it, we're going to be clobbered." This attack turned out to be the Tet offensive, and even if Allen was wrong about the nationality of the attackers, she was right that the attack would occur. Allen believed that if MACV paid attention to her report then, "all those people wouldn't have been dead." [1]

Allen's warning about Tet was not the only time intelligence officers ignored Allen's reports. On another occasion, her sources indicated that the Viet Cong would ambush a certain convoy: when the command ignored this report, five soldiers died and another 19 were injured. Even after intelligence officers asked Allen for information, many of them sought further confirmation of Allen's reports. Allen saw prejudices throughout her time in Vietnam, "Black, woman- got no business here. WAC, you're not supposed to be in the army- this is a man's job."[2]

Allen, an intelligence analyst who was ignored and second-guessed, details a specific problem in the study of the Vietnam War. As a woman, and a minority, her function as a soldier in Vietnam was undervalued. Scholars of the Vietnam War, and of the Women's Army Corps, while covering commissioned nurses, often neglect to cover the enlisted woman's roles in Vietnam. Historiography of women in the Vietnam War often ignores the roles of these non-medical personnel in favor of nursing personnel for two reasons: first, the only female deaths in Vietnam were nurses, and secondly, nursing as an extension of woman's role as caregiver.

The small number of American military women in Vietnam, combined with the restriction that barred women from serving in combat positions, marginalized their contribution to the military effort and amplified the struggle for the female Vietnam veteran to achieve recognition as a veteran. The performance of women in non-combative military occupational specialties in Vietnam showed the military branches that women could perform in greater roles and numbers while the military prepared for a move towards an all-volunteer force.

This research explores the role of enlisted servicewomen in Vietnam, primarily the Women's Army Corps (WACs), the largest female service organization, at Long Binh. First, by examining government publications, I will detail the extent of the WAC in Vietnam, including how many served, and what military occupational specialties were filled by WACs in the war, and recruitment strategies of the Women's Army Corps.

Second, by examining oral histories and scholarly works, I will discuss the servicewomen's experience in Vietnam, comparing the stories with that of men in the rear echelon and in combat units. For my final section, I will discuss the female soldier's interactions with the men, the WAC contribution and influence of the WACs to the military, and the struggle to gain recognition as Veterans.

You mean women served too?

Lena Allred estimated that, of the 7,500 to 11,000 American military women who served in Vietnam, 1,300 of were in non-medical professions.[3] In 1972, the *New York Times* estimated that there were "about 13,000 WACs [and] at least 160 in Vietnam."[4] From 1966-1972, 700 WAC soldiers served in Vietnam, with no fatalities, no MIAs and no reported POWs; only one WAC, SP5c Sheron L Green, received the Purple Heart. By contrast, eight female nurses died in Vietnam from 1963-1973, but these women were the only deaths.[5] The higher number of medical servicewomen and the fact that nurses died while non-medical women survived attributes to the struggle for non-medical servicewomen to gain scholarly recognition.

The very first WAC in Vietnam was M/Sgt Florence E. Friedman, secretary to Maj. Gen. Robert M. Montague, when she followed Gen. Montague to Saigon in 1955.[6] In 1964, a personnel officer in Headquarters, MACV wrote the WAC director that the Republic of Vietnam was organizing a Women's Armed Forces Corps (WAFC) and MACV thought that the WACs should help organize this force; this program ultimately trained fifty-one Vietnamese female officers.[7] The New York Times reported that the first two women to train the WAFC, Maj. Kathleen I. Wilkes and SFC Betty Adams, arrived in Vietnam on January 15, 0 1965.[8] In 1965, General William Westmoreland (1914-2005) requested fifteen WAC stenographers who had achieved the rank of E-5 or higher for MACV, in 1970 this stenographer pool peaked at 23 in 1970.[9] In 1966, United States Army Vietnam (USARV) deputy commander, Lt. Gen. Jean E Engler, requested a 50 (later 100) member WAC detachment consisting of clerk/typists and administration workers , and a cadre to lead the WAC unit.[10] By January of 1970, WAC presence in Vietnam peaked at 20 officers, 139 enlisted women (with 54 officers and 393 women in the Pacific theater).[11] Rhodri Jeffries-Jones stated the highest estimate of women who served in Vietnam was 55,000, with 80% serving as nurses, and explained that women who "were barred from combat failed to experience the horror of the war firsthand."[12]

Vietnam-era Servicewomen were very limited in their military occupational specialties (MOS). The 1963 *Report of the Committee on Federal Employment* for the U.S Presidential Commission on the Status of Women, reported 28 "enlisted occupations," most of which were medical or clerical, though a few other listed careers included musician, Air Traffic Control, recruiter, and photographer.[13] Women Marines filled 20 occupations, mostly clerical and logistic jobs. [14] Naval enlisted women were limited to medical career choices.[15] Women enlisted in the Women's Air Force (WAF) had choices that allowed them to be illustrators, cartographers, communication center operators, or work in Air operations.[16] In 1972, the *New York Times* reported that women filled 150 MOSes, including "electronics, graphics, medical, [and] food service."[17] In 1970, WAC strength in Vietnam was at its peak, MOSes included communication specialists, personnel, finance, data processing, and intelligence along with the clerk/typist/stenographer roles.[18]

Table 1: Women in the Military		
Service	Sept, 1962[19]	June 1970[20]
Army	9,673	16,724
Navy	6,233	8,254
Air Force	5,583	13,787
Marines	1,712	2,418

Although the few numbers of women serving in the military during the Vietnam War marginalized their role in the war, military service for women expanded in the Vietnam era. As can be seen in table one, all of the branches of service showed an increase in personnel during the 1960s. In 1962, men outnumbered women in the military 70:1, in 1972 that ratio lowered to 43:1.[21] From WWII to 1973, the military had a 2% quota for women, a quota that the military had a difficult time meeting, even with the rise of uniformed women throughout the 1960s.[22] Because the women were all volunteers, recruitment and retention were high priorities for the female military services. There were stricter standards for women to enter the military: a woman had to be a high school graduate, provide character references, and have personal interviews to enter the WAC.[23] As late as 1973, women who wished to join needed parental permission if they were younger than 21 (compared to 18 for men), and were required to have higher testing scores than men to enter.[24] In 1966, the Department of Defense called for a 38% extension of the Women's Army Corps to help support the war.[25] In 1967, the US Army Recruiting Command wanted to increase annual WAC enlistment from 4,000 to 6,000. [26] Despite the growth of the women's services, none of the branches met enlistment goals during the 1960s; hostility toward the Vietnam War affected recruiting. In 1966, the WAC eliminated mandatory discharge on marriage, in hopes to lessen loss of strength; losses dropped by 7% for marriage, but women seeking discharge used other methods.[27]

It is interesting to note that although the Air Force had fewer women than the Army, the Air Force had a higher concentration of female service members because the branch had the fewest combat roles. [28] As of 1969, only the Air Force fully admitted women into its Reserve Officers Training Corps (ROTC) program. In that year, the Air Force had 6 female cadets training in drill, parachuting, and make-up techniques. This program was an "experiment" to attract coeds during a time when "male disillusionment with the Vietnam War thinned the ranks" of Air Force ROTC.[29] The first group of female cadets in the Air Force ROTC was all white, middle-class, one, Cadet Leslie Farr, was the daughter of an Air Force Colonel. Jon Nordheimer stated that all of the female cadets "join[ed] the program because of a desire to travel and an ambition to do more than 'getting married and having kids.'"

One method used by the WAC to assist recruitment was a touring informational exhibit on the

Corps. This exhibit was first led by Lt. Col (later Brig. Gen.) Mildred Inez Caroon Bailey, who was chief of WAC recruiting for the Third US Army from 1958-1961.[30] Brig. Gen. Bailey explained that during her time in recruiting, she had some successes "selling" the WAC through television and radio, and said that when WAC director Col. Emily C Gorman assigned her to the exhibit, the director explained:

We feel we should send somebody who's had a few years of military service, who's more mature, settled, married, to see what the problems are going to be when you're traveling the country as a team. We think you're the one for it because of all the experience you've had in recruiting and the television and the radio.[31]

Bailey found that the initial set-up for the exhibit left a lot of free time for the soldiers touring with the exhibit, and designed a "fashion show." The exhibit displayed not just 1960s WAC uniforms as well as uniforms for army women from the beginning of the WAC, uniforms of "Yeomanette, the Marinette, and the nurse in World War I," but also nurses' uniforms from the Spanish-American War.[32] The WACs on the exhibit were to answer questions about life as a WAC, and had model training before joining the team; the exhibit tour was limited to six months so the soldiers would not spend too much time working outside their MOS.[33] Bailey explained that a major reason she was told that women joined was "I like the uniform."[34] Brig. Gen. Bailey explained that during her time in the military, whenever she was in uniform, she remained in uniform, even while on a plane:

I wouldn't even take my hat off or unbutton my blouse even if it was a twelve-hour flight, because I'm a woman in uniform. If I'm sloppy with my blouse undone and my hair in a mess, that is for every woman in uniform. They will judge every woman in uniform by that.[35]

General Bailey was aware that while wearing the uniform, people were watching her, judging all servicewomen by what they saw in her. She remained in her feminine uniform to show that women in the military were ladies. This, in part, was to counter the public image and stereotype of the female soldier as a lesbian, whore, or a "loser looking for a husband."[36]

Although this exhibit may have helped recruitment, the fashion show aspect of the exhibit is part of an early trend of studying women in the US military forces. A large amount of press for women in the military discussed what the women wore. Virginia Lee Warren devoted three long paragraphs to the early WAC uniforms in her 1972 *New York Times* article "The WAC: Born in Time of Crisis and Still Flourishing." Jon Nordheimer's 1969 *New York Times* article about women in the Air Force ROTC program is entitled, "Lipstick is part of Uniform." When the Air Force planned to send women to Vietnam, the *Washington Post* published an article titled "No Limp Fatigues for WAFS in Viet," discussing the uniforms Air Force women would wear in Vietnam. The WAFS would not wear "baggy green fatigues," but instead "a short-sleeve blouse, a wrap-around skirt, and comfortable kind of shoe for walking in sand."[37] Even a March 2009 article in *Soldiers* Magazine about the Women's Army Corps devoted a lot of time to the uniforms, make-up requirements, and poor-quality field boots issued to WAC members.[38]

Focusing on the fashion of women in the military as a recruitment strategy may have been a way to show a positive WAC image to potential recruits and their families. With both the recruiting strategy and newspaper articles, the focus on the female uniform was a way to keep the women, working in traditionally "masculine" roles as soldiers, connected with a feminine image. Nordheimer described Cadet Farr as "honey blond," and "5 feet 3 inches [weighing] 99 pounds."[39] Dorothy McCardle described Women's Air Force director Col Jeanne C. Holm as "slim, trim and dynamic" who "wore a skirt every place [she] went in Vietnam, and saw no reason why WAFS stationed out there can't wear skirts, too."[40] WACs in Vietnam initially wore the "green cord" uniform while on duty, but after the Tet offensive, they wore lightweight fatigues.[41]

While Allred explained that a majority of works about the Vietnam War "ignore[d] the effect of war on . . . the American women who also served," she still failed to recognize that most of the works focused on nurses instead of enlisted women.[42] Most of the books and memoirs discussed by Allred were about or by nurses. Allred discussed that fictional literature about American servicewomen in Vietnam consists of "adolescent nurse novels, romance novels, or adult fiction bordering on or blatantly pornographic" and included "thinly drawn stereotypes" of women.[43] The women in Vietnam literature were "background figures," and many women who served "could not overcome the gender stereotyping."[44] While Allred mentioned that the scholarship marginalizes the roles of women who served in Vietnam and discussed that the greater numbers of nurses over non-medical servicewomen, most of her source material covered the nurse and medical servicewomen.

Who were these women?

Thus far, I have examined the strength of women in the armed services during Vietnam, military specialties available to women in the military, and discussed recruitment of women to the military services. Now, I shall examine the women who served: why they joined, what they experienced in Vietnam, and compare their stories to male service members in both combat and rear echelon roles in Vietnam.

In his book *Working-Class War: American Combat Soldiers and Vietnam,* Christian G. Appy stated that roughly 1/3 of all soldiers were draftees, 1/3 were draft-motivated volunteers, and the final 1/3 of male soldiers in the U.S. Armed services were actual volunteers for service.[45] Throughout *Working-Class War,* Appy discussed the demographics of male soldiers in Vietnam as overwhelmingly working class, young, and from minority backgrounds. Women serving in Vietnam were typically older, middle class, had higher education, and were white.[46]

Many of the new soldiers saw "no real or attractive alternative" to joining the service.[47] In 1968, 30% of volunteers surveyed said they "wanted [their] choice of service rather than to be drafted" 17% replied they joined to "fulfill my military obligation," 11% joined to "learn a trade that would be valuable in civilian life," and only 6% joined for pure patriotism.[48] Allred detailed that nurses who joined made their decisions for many of the same reasons, but also for "feminine" reasons, "to provide nurture to the fighting men, boost their morale, and heal their broken bodies and spirits."[49] Jeffries-Jones explained that the nurses "who enjoyed themselves… boosted military morale and contributed to the military cause."[50]

There were a number of motivating factors for women to enlist (or accept a commission) within the armed forces during the Vietnam era. One of the primary reasons may have been that men and women in the military received equal pay based on their ranks, though women did not receive special bonuses like those received by pilots/flight crews in the Air Force.[51] WAC members began drawing equal pay with men as early as 1942.[52] Equal pay may have been a very strong motivating factor for women to seek employment in the armed forces. In 1969, Air Force Cadet Farr explained:

I'm not a champion of women's rights. . . but I don't think I should have to suffer because I'm a female, that I should receive lower pay in private industry just because of my sex.[53]

Women who joined the Women's Army Corps had reasons to join other than financial reasons. Doris "Lucki" Allen joined in 1950, in part because her brother was a World-War II veteran.[54] Karen Offut, a stenographer, joined at age 19 because she "believed in what we were doing. That we were fighting communism and trying to help these people that were oppressed."[55]

Marilyn Roth joined in 1964 because "I'd get an education, and experience."[56] Captain (later Lt. Col.) Nancy Jurgevich joined "right out of high school . . . in 1958" because her small town had few options and "I wanted to travel."[57] Audrey Ann Fisher (1926-) joined in 1949 for patriotic reasons, and because of a desire to see the world.[58] Charlotte Holder Clinger joined the Air Force in 1967 because she could not make a living as a teacher and because she told her Air Force recruiter she would join "If you get my brother out of the draft, and you get me Intelligence."[59] Dorothy Rechel joined in 1953 because "All I ever really wanted to do was be in the Army, and I don't know why that is."[60]

They all volunteered to go to Vietnam. All of these women served in Vietnam. Offut believed in the war, and begged to go to Vietnam, and served from 1969-170. Roth went because she wanted to be adventurous.[61] Fisher did not explain why she wanted to go to Vietnam. [62] Rechel went because she saw herself "as a career type- absolutely committed," and when you are a career military person, you were supposed to go to war.[63]

Arriving in Vietnam was harsh for all soldiers. Appy described the confusion of soldiers first entering Vietnam, the use of commercial jets starting in 1966, and the increased business of Tan Son Nhut airbase in the 1960s.[64] Soldiers arriving often wanted to return home when they arrived, jealous of homecoming soldiers, alarmed by the appearance of the returning soldiers; the returning soldiers were excited to see their "Freedom Birds."[65] Both Roth and Offut remembered their planes landing to a crowd of shouts, the planes they landed in were planes that were taking soldiers home, Freedom Birds.[66] The female soldiers entering Vietnam certainly felt all the same anxieties as the male soldiers with an added difference. While the male soldiers were traveling with the men from units they either had already served with or were about to serve with, the women often were traveling alone, without other females from their unit. This gave the women feelings of isolation added to the anxieties of flying into a war zone.

Doris Allen arrived in a plane with "two-hundred-and-something men . . .and me;" Allen was the only new arrival wearing a Class A uniform.[67] Although many newspapers paid heavy attention to the uniforms worn by female military personnel in Vietnam, very few of them considered the uniform in context of the climate of Vietnam. With high humidity and temperatures that often reached above 100°F, Vietnam was not a comfortable environment for the wool class-A uniform.[68] The wool class-A uniform covered the women in sweat when they arrived in Vietnam; without fatigues, the WACs were uncomfortable.[69] With the high concentration of orange dust and mud in Vietnam, it was hard for the WAC soldiers to remain "ladies" and look "just perfect."[70] When given the choice of fatigues or the green cord uniform, most women chose to wear fatigues.[71]

The Army billeted the first WACs in Vietnam in various, non air-conditioned hotel rooms in Saigon. Despite the Army's insistence that the WACs would be stationed in non-combat zones, Saigon was not a safe environment; the bus the WACs rode to work was firebombed (while empty), and women also worried about the threat of bombs on the street.[72] When General Engler requested his WAC detachment, he decided to house his WACs in a military containment area at Tan Son Nhut to avoid using extra guards to protect the female soldiers. The WACS would receive training in "small weapons" if, and only if, they were assigned to field installations.[73] In December of 1968, the WAC detachment moved to permanent barracks at Long Binh. The WAC billets consisted of four two-story wooden buildings that had areas for cooking and laundry, a swimming pool, and planned capacity was for up to 130 women. The rooms averaged 20'x36' and housed 4-5 women per room, and were air-conditioned.[74]

The detachment quarters in Long Binh was fenced-in, and had a guard detail stationed around it 24-hours a day, every day. Women had to get approval to go anywhere outside of the living quarters. Women could only leave secure area "if you had official business to go to, or if some boss of yours would say, 'Let's go to Saigon for the day;'" trips to Saigon required permission from the high command and "two men with two weapons."[75] Roth explained that the constant protection and guard at Long Binh, "wasn't jail, but it felt like it."[76] Further security included 10:30 bed checks every night. Roth remembers a "reactionary force" of infantrymen that protected the WAC women "all the time. That was their main job. . ."[77] This close-quarters allowed Roth to feel "protected, secure, and very special" and "I never felt that camaraderie and that closeness with anybody in my entire life."[78] The few married WACS who went to Vietnam often tried to get assigned near their military husbands, but often found that there was no family quarters and that their husbands' stations were far away. In May of 1969, the US Army made a policy to ban married WACs from serving in Vietnam if they had spouses already in Vietnam; this was in response to complaints from civilian wives who "could not even travel there."[79]

Despite this comfortable description of the women's barracks, the WACs did not necessarily remember being comfortable or safe within their living quarters. The VC often tried to take over Long Binh to gain access to food supplies and the post suffered rocket fire on a regular basis.[80] Long Binh was also not the only place WAC soldiers lived. Karen Offut, who only spent a short time at Long Binh, spent most of her time in Saigon, living in a hotel. Most of the women in Saigon were older, and Offut did not see other WAC soldiers much throughout the day. The guards for the Saigon women were ARVN, and Offut "didn't really feel safe no matter where [she] went."[81] Nancy Jurgevich, as a commander, felt that her soldiers did not always take the threat seriously. During one alert, some of the soldiers were more concerned with preparing food and a picnic than grabbing the necessary helmets and canteens. [82]

Offut's expression of not feeling safe while in Vietnam proved that even people serving in "non-combat roles" could feel threatened while serving in a war zone. Appy explained the danger of the rear-echelon, where all WACs served. Even soldiers who were not in combat zones felt the threat of death, and could be preoccupied with the dangers in Vietnam, and feel the fear of dying.[83] Although Appy did include discussion of servicewomen and this discussion of rear-echelon dangers, he did not include women in the discussion of rear-echelon fear. Appy said "Every *man* had to find some way to explain, accept, deflect, or escape the presence of death."[84] Allen found her name on a list of people the North Vietnamese wanted dead, and began carrying a weapon because of the fear of attack.[85] Offut remembered being terrified during bombings, but eventually "got used to it."[86] Offut explained that "You go from a child more or less to an adult, almost instantly . . . you had to step out of your youth and your childhood to be able to accept it and to endure it."[87] Being in the rear echelon also did not mean a soldier did not get exposed to Agent Orange; Audrey Fisher would often see Agent Orange dripping from the planes that returned from defoliating missions.[88]

Appy believed that the morale in the rear echelon for soldiers was not high. Rear echelon forces experienced:

More racial conflicts, higher levels of excessive drinking and drug use, fuller exposure to black marketeering and political corruption, and deeper subjection to petty military regulations and the authority of officers.[89]

Appy did not look at the morale of female soldiers, who certainly may have faced some of these problems. In 1967, Col. Elizabeth P. Hoisington, then Director of the Women's Army Corps, visited her troops in Vietnam, and found that the WACs had high morale, were satisfied with their work, had commanders and supervisors interested in their health and well-being, and were well-housed, well-clothed, and well-fed.[90] While it is possible that the Director's presence increased the morale of the women, it is possible that the women did have higher morale. Nancy Jurgevich explained that while her soldiers worked 12 hour days, 7 days a week, her soldiers "loved their jobs . . .[And] liked being there."[91] Offut, with her feelings of isolation and fear, did not have high morale. Roth, who spent time off duty going to clubs, dancing, and "hav[ing] a nice time" had a higher morale. [92] Female soldiers' narratives show that while the command believed the women had a higher morale, and it is true that some of the women did have good morale while serving in Vietnam, that was not the case for every soldier.

Ignorance and Influence

So, I have looked at the demographics of the women who served in Vietnam and I have relayed a few stories of their time in Vietnam and discussed morale amongst WAC members. After returning from the war, friends and family did not want to hear the war stories of women, and they were "brushed off" by friends, male veterans, and the Veteran's Administration (VA).[93] This section explores why it is important to study the stories of these women, how they have been ignored as Veterans and their value as rear echelon soldiers.

The WACs in Vietnam proved that they could work efficiently in a war-zone and work professionally alongside male soldiers. While General Bailey believed that American society would never accept the idea of women training for and participating in combat, service in Vietnam proved that women could serve in dangerous areas.[94] Jurgevich certainly believed that her soldiers in Vietnam contributed to the war effort.[95] Whether they were typing secret crypto messages like Marilyn Roth, preparing intelligence documents like Doris Allen, or taking dictation from officers to detail orders to the troops, all of the women performed their roles admirably.[96] Gen. Engler felt that the WAC service in Vietnam was "superb" and further explained:

[The WACs] handled clerical and management assignments in headquarters Vietnam in an outstanding manner. It would have been a serious mistake not to use their skills. The decision to employ WAC's in Vietnam was correct.[97]

Gen. Engler, who requested the WAC detachment of stenographers, only considered the performance of the clerical workers and not the intelligence workers. The jobs all the women did were important, just as the jobs performed in the rear-echelon by non-combative male soldiers were important; the non-combative forces were support for the focus, the fighting forces.

While investigating the possible ramifications of women in the military for the ERA, a senate Judiciary report stated that women "have demonstrated that they can perform admirably in many capacities in the armed forces" and that women and men would "not [be] required to serve where not fitted."[98] Vietnam proved that women could serve in combat-areas.

Air Force Cadet Farr's lack of identification with the women's rights movement fit the scholarship of women's rights and the military during the 1960s. A disconnect occurs when studying women's rights and the armed forces. Very few of the women who the military recruited during the Vietnam era seem to have identified themselves with the women's liberation movement. Goldman theorized that women in the military simply "[were] not attached to the militant women's liberation movement."[99] In *Peace Now!* Rhodri Jeffries-Jones explained that while women initially supported the war because of "gender-specific ideological reasons," American women have generally "been more antiwar than American men.[100] Jeffries-Jones also explained, "in the sixties . . . most women preferred not to be involved in feminism or other radical causes."[101]

Books on the women's rights movement also shows a disconnect between women and the military. In her book *No Turning Back: The History of Feminism and the Future of Women,* Estelle B. Freedman did not discuss female roles in the military and instead focused on pacifist movements like the Women Strike for Peace.[102] Paula Giddings' *When and Where I Enter: The Impact of Black Women on Race and Sex in America* talks in depth about women in the Civil Rights movement, but ignores the Vietnam war altogether. *Through Women's Eyes: an American History with Documents* by Ellen Carol Dubois and Lynn Dumenil discussed women in the military during WWII, and briefly discussed women in the anti-war movement, but no mention of women serving during the Vietnam War.[103] In *The World Split Open: How the Modern Women's Movement Changed America*, Ruth Rosen gave a brief discussion on women in the anti-war movement, but, again, did not discuss women serving in the military.[104] These books show a pattern of disconnect between the women's movement and 1960s female soldiers.

When the women's liberation movement did look at women in the military, it was in the context of equality with men in the military. Leaders demanded women have the same criteria for entry as men, that women be allowed to enter the service academies alongside men, and that restrictions against women in combat be removed. Women's liberation leaders also asked for the end of separate women's military organizations.[105] General Bailey remembered:

I could see that unless we were totally integrated into the system with the same rules, same regulations, same opportunities, we were going nowhere. And yet we had a nice comfortable existence where we were. We had our own history. No, it's not infantry history and it's not artillery history; but it's our history and you hate to give that up.[106]

In a 1987 letter to the editor of the *New York Times*, Barbara L. Shay, a former military nurse, said that it was "unfortunate that the movement to add a female figure to the Vietnam War memorial was initiated by a nurse." Shay said that she believed that a nurse-led movement to add a women's memorial "may obscure the fact that all specialties in the services have increasingly been shared by both sexes."[107] The nurse-led movement would undercut the roles performed by all the rear echelon, not just the female soldiers. Shay was correct in her supposition. Lynda Van DeVanter (1947-2002), who headed the push for the Vietnam Women's Memorial believed that the women who served as nurses were the "most forgotten" veterans.[108] Marilyn Roth has a license plate stating, "Served in Vietnam" and has often been asked if she was a Nurse. When she replies that she was not, the inquisitive "wouldn't even talk to me. . . They don't care about us. Basically, they know nurses."[109] As a civilian, Karen Offut studied to become a Nurse; when people discover she was in Vietnam, they "think I was automatically a nurse."[110] Offut felt that because she was not a nurse in Vietnam, they thought, "it didn't count," and personally did not feel "that I really was validated by going over there."[111] Van DeVanter was wrong, nurses were not the most forgotten, the enlisted women were. Nurses were performing roles that expressed feminine traits: looking towards the health and well-being of combat-injured troops, thus the nurse's role in Vietnam is deemed important enough to remember. Nursing "counts," typing intelligence documents does not.

VanDevanter was correct in her statement that no women were studied in Agent Orange exposure studies and to inform the public of women's post-traumatic stress disorder (PTSD) because of Vietnam.[112] The press given to nurses experiencing PTSD does not give due attention to the non-nurses experiencing PTSD. Allen and Offut both experienced PTSD.[113] Without ever serving in a combat role, Offut still experienced a Vietnam war that made her reluctant to form close relationships, fearful of everything around her, and in a constant state of hyper-vigilance.[114] Van DeVanter explained that nurses often feared having children for fear of birth defects.[115] Offut's three children all had medical disabilities- Cancer, epilepsy, and ADHD; Offut blamed her Agent Orange exposure for her children's illnesses.[116]

Perhaps the problem with scholars and society recognizing women veterans stems from the voluntary nature of their service. All of the women serving in Vietnam volunteered, so any post-war problems they experienced were because of volunteering. Had they not volunteered, they would not experience PTSD, would not have been exposed to Agent Orange, and would not have birth defects in their children. This was certainly the attitude of Karen Offut's (ex) husband, who blamed her for volunteering, and by association thus blamed Karen for their children's illnesses.[117] Because the women *volunteered* to go into the army, *volunteered* to take the traditional "man's role," they were blamed for any personal consequences as a result for volunteering. Because few of the military women were associated with the women's rights movement, they lacked the social network involved with membership in women's organizations like NOW or LWV.[118] Without that network, the military women lacked a forum, and no way to show that they were being blamed for their wartime stresses because they entered the 'man's world' of the military.

The strongest influence of female Vietnam enlisted veterans was that their experiences showed women could perform productively within an All-Volunteer force. Morris Janowitz theorized that the new, all-volunteer force would work, even if the military had to lower standards for recruitment and retention and lower the level of military personnel.[119] The military had difficulty in recruiting personnel in adequate numbers and of adequate quality.[120] Janowitz conceded that women would be necessary to fill the ranks of the all-volunteer force, but theorized that women would never comprise more than 10% of the US military forces.[121] After the draft ended, the army wanted to double the strength of the WAC before 1978.[122] When General Bailey was assigned to be the WAC director, General Westmoreland told her, "you've got to get the public support for when we start trying to recruit thousands of more women."[123] Had women not served in Vietnam, there would have been great doubts in the mind of the military of increasing womanpower in the military, even with the necessity of women in the all-volunteer army, because the projected totals of 10% could not help make up the numbers of men lost to military service because they were not drafted.

Women have served with the U.S. military since the beginning of the United States. From the founding of the Women's Army Corps in 1945 to its integration into the U.S. Army in 1978, WACs have served honorably in the military, often with very little recognition, but with equal pay with men. History remembers WACs for their service in World War II, but unfairly forgets their service afterwards, especially for their service in Vietnam. In a time of domestic conflict over a controversial war, these women volunteered. They volunteered for the Army. They volunteered for Vietnam and, were put aside and forgotten about, because they did noncombative non-maternal jobs.

Works Cited

Primary Sources

Allen, Doris "Lucki." "Doris 'Lucki' Allen, WAC (Women's Army Corps)." In *Women in Vietnam* by Ron Steinman, 241-254. New York: TV Books, 2000.

Department of Labor, Women's Bureau, Citizens Advisory Council and Interdepartmental Committee on the Status of Women. "Women in the Military." in *Women in 1973* by Department of Labor, Women's Bureau, Citizens Advisory Council and Interdepartmental Committee on the Status of Women, 17-19.Washington, DC: U.S> Government Printing Office, 1974.

Gutwillig, Jacqueline G. "Equal rights Amendment Jubilee-Ratification Assembly, May 10, 1972." in *Women in 1972* by Citizens' Advisory Council on the Status of Women, 44-48. Washington, DC: U.S. Government Printing office, 1973.

Jurgevich, Nancy. "Nancy Jurgevich, WAC (Women's Army Corps)" in *Women in Vietnam*, 233-240.

Montana Department of Labor and Industry Research and Analysis Bureau. "Armed Forces/Veterans." in *Montana Women in the 80's* by Montana Department of Labor and Industry Research and Analysis Bureau, 62-65. Helena, MT. 1985.

Morden, Bettie J. *The Women's Army Corps, 1945-1978* . Washington, D.C.: Center of Military History, United States Army, 19990. *This book is a military-produced book about the history of the Women's Army Corps, written by a WAC who served throughout the history of the Corps. I include it as a Primary Source for this very reason.*

Offut, Karen. "Karen Offut WAC (Women's Army Corps) Stenographer, MACV." In *Women in Vietnam*, 254-269.

Roth, Marilyn. "Marilyn Roth, WAC (Women's Army Corps)" in *Women in Vietnam*, 223-232.

U. S. President' Committee on the Status of Women. *Report of the Committee on Federal Employment.* Washington, DC: U.S. Government Printing Office, 1963.

Oral Histories

Bailey, General Mildred Inez Caroon. Interview with Eric Elliott. May 26,1999. Object WV0084.5.001, transcript. Women Veterans Historical Collection. Greensboro, NC: University of North Carolina-Greensboro.
http://library.uncg.edu/dp/wv/results5.aspx?i=2017&s=5

Clinger, Charlotte Holder. Interview with Beth Carmichael. August 8, 2006. Object WV023.5.001, transcript. University of North-Carolina, Greensboro.
http://library.uncg.edu/dp/wv/results5.aspx?i=2701&s=5&c=4

Fisher, Audrey Ann. Interview with Eric Elliott. December 18, 2000. Object WV0153.2.001, transcript. University of North-Carolina, Greensboro.
http://library.uncg.edu/dp/wv/results5.aspx?i=2661&s=5&c=4

Rechel, Dorothy Jane. Interview with Eric Elliott. January 22, 2001. Object WE0196.5.001, transcript. University of North-Carolina, Greensboro.
http://library.uncg.edu/dp/wv/results5.aspx?i=2930&s=5&c=4

Newspapers

"2 WACS Arrive in Saigon." *New York Times,* January 16, 1965. p 11.

"Army Woman Assigned to Service in Saigon." *New York Times.* May 1, 1955. p 80.

Dullea, Georgia. "Like Men Who Fought, They Tell ofAnxiety and Painful Recall." *New York Times.* May 23, 1981, A1..

McCardle, Dorothy. "No Limp Fatigues for WAFS in Vietnam." *Washington Post.* February 8,1967, B4.

Nordheimer, Jon. "Lipstick Is Part of Uniform." *New York Times.* December 17, 1969, p 37.

Shay, Barbara L. "A Time to Recognize that Women are Veterans Too." *New York Times.* October 28,1987, A30.

Warren, Virginia Lee. "The WAC: Born in Time of Crisis and Still Flourishing. *New York Times.* May 7, 1972. p 83.

Secondary

Allred, Lena. "Women in a Man's World: American Women in the Vietnam War." In *The Vietnam War: Handbook of the Literature and Research* edited by James S. Olson, 303-317. Westport, Ct: Greenwood Press, 1993.

Appy, Christian G. *Working Class War: American Combat Soldiers and Vietnam.* Chapel Hill, NC: University of North Carolina Press, 1993.

Collins, Elizabeth. "Remembering the Women's Army Corps." *Soldiers.* (March, 2009), 4-9.

Dubois, Ellen Carol and Lynn Dumenil. *Through Women's Eyes: An American History with Documents.* New York: Bedford/St. Martin's, 2000.

Freedman, Estelle B. *No Turning Back: The History of Feminism and the Future of Women.* New York: Ballantine Books, 2002.

Goldman, Nancy. "The Changing Role of Women in the Armed Forces" in "Changing Women in a Changing Society." Special Issue, *American Journal of Sociology* 78 no 4, (January 1973), 892-911.

Janowitz, Morris. "The All-Volunteer Military as a 'Sociopolitical' Problem" in *Social Problems* Vol 22, no 3 (Feb 1975), 432-449.

Jeffries-Jones, Rhodri. *Peace Now! American Society and the Ending of the Vietnam War.* New Haven: Yale University Press, 1999.

Mithers, Carol Lynn. "Missing in Action: Women Warriors in Vietnam." In "American Representations of Vietnam," Special Issue, *Cultural Critique* no 3 (Spring, 1986), 79-90.

Endnotes

[1] Doris Allen, "Doris 'Lucki' Allen, WAC (Women's Army Corps" in *Women in Vietnam* by Ron Steinman (New York: TV Books, 2000), 241, 245, 246-7.

[2] Allen, 243-44.

[3] Lena Allred, "Women in a Man's World: American Women in the Vietnam War," in *The Vietnam War: Handbook of the Literature and Research* ed. James S Olson (Westport, Ct: Greenwood Press, 1993) 303.

[4] Virginia Lee Warren, "The WAC: Born in Time of Crisis and Still Flourishing," *New York Times* May 7, 1972 p 83.

[5] Bettie J Morden, *The Women's Army Corps, 1945-1978* (Washington, D.C: Center of Military History, United States Army, 1990), 254.

[6] "Army Woman Assigned to Service in Saigon," *New York Times* May 1, 1955, p 80.

[7] Morden, 242-243.

[8] "2 WACS Arrive in Saigon," *New York Times*, January 16, 1965p 11.

[9] Morden, 243.

[10] Morden, 245.

[11] Morden, 248.

[12] Rhodri Jeffries-Jones, *Peace Now! American Society and the Ending of the Vietnam War* (New Haven: Yale University Press, 1999), 145.

[13] U. S. President' Committee on the Status of Women, *Report of the Committee on Federal Employment*, (Washington, DC: U.S. Government Printing Office, 1963),187.

[14] Ibid., 188.

[15] Ibid., 190.

[16] Ibid., 185.

[17] Warren.

[18] Morden, 248-9.

[19] U.S. President's Committee on the Status of Women, 184.

[20] Department of Labor, "Women in the Military,"17.

[21] Montana Department of Labor and Industry Research and Analysis Bureau, "Armed Forces/Veterans,"in *Montana Women in the 80's* Montana Department of Labor and Industry Research and Analysis Bureau (Helena, MT, 1985) 62.

[22]Nancy Goldman, "The Changing Role of Women in the Armed Forces," in "Changing women in a changing Society," special issue, *American Journal of Sociology* 78 no 4, (January 1973) 892. A 1971 study by the US Army called for an end to the @5 ceiling, stating that 20-35% of military positions could be filled by women. (897).

[23] Jacqueline G. Gutwillig, "Equal rights Amendment Jubilee-Ratification Assembly, May 10, 1972," in *Women in 1972* by Citizens' Advisory Council on the Status of Women (Washington, DC: U.S Government Printing office, 1973),, 45.

[24] Department of Labor, Women's Bureau, Citizens Advisory Council and Interdepartmental Committee on the Status of Women, "Women in the Military," in *Women in 1973,* by Department of Labor, Women's Bureau, Citizens Advisory Council and Interdepartmental Committee on the Status of Women (Washington, DC: U.S> Government Printing Office, 1974), 18

[25] Morden, 219.

[26] Ibid., 224.

[27] Ibid., 225-6.

[28] Goldman, 901.

[29] Jon Nordheimer, "Lipstick Is Part of Uniform," *New York Times* December 17, 1969, p 37.

[30] General Mildred Inez Caroon Bailey, interview with Eric Elliott,May 26, 1999, Object WV0084.5.001, transcript, Women Veterans Historical Collection, University of North Carolina-Greensboro, Greensboro, NC. http://library.uncg.edu/dp/wv/results5.aspx?i=2017&s=5 . Third Army was responsible for recruiting throughout the southeast.

[31] Bailey, interview.

[32] Bailey, interview.

[33] Morden, 191.

[34] Bailey, interview.

[35] Bailey, interview.

[36] Carol Lynn Mithers, "Missing in Action: Women Warriors in Vietnam," in "American Representations of Vietnam," special issue, *Cultural Critique no 3,* (Spring, 1986), 81.

[37] Dorothy McCardle, "No Limp Fatigues for WAFS in Vietnam," *Washington Post* February 8, 1967 p B4.

[38] Elizabeth M. Collins, "Remembering the Women's Army Corps," *Soldiers* (March, 2009), 6. A later part of the article detailed how, after 1975 when women were permitted to remain in the military during pregnancy, there was no uniform for the woman.

[39] Nordheimer.

[40] McCardle.

[41] Morden, 244.

[42] Allred, 303.

[43] Allred, 309.

[44] Allred, 304.

[45] Christian G. Appy, *Working Class War: American Comabt Soldiers and Vietnam* (Chapel Hill, University of North Carolina Press, 1993), 28.

[46]Mithers, 79.

[47] Appy, 44.

[48] Appy, 46. I could not find statistical data like Appy's applying only to female volunteers during the Vietnam war.

[49] Allred, 307.

[50] Jeffries-Jones, 146.

[51] Nordheimer, "Lipstick."

[52] Morden, 5.

[53] Nordheimer, "Lipstick."

[54] Allen, 242.

[55] Karren Offut, "Karen Offut WAC (Women's Army Corps) Stenographer, MACV" in *Women in Vietnam*, 254.

[56] Marilyn Roth, "Marilyn Roth, WAC (Women's Army Corps)" in *Women in the Vietnam*, 224.

[57] Nancy Jurgevich, "Nancy Jurgevich WAC (Women's Army Corps)" in *Women in Vietnam*, 240. Jurgevich spent time in Vietnam as WAC Detachment Commander in 1968

[58] Audrey Ann Fisher, interview with Eric Elliott, December 18, 2000, Object WV0153.5.001, transcript, Women Veterans Historical Collection, University of North Carolina-Greensboro, Greensboro, NC.
http://library.uncg.edu/dp/wv/results5.aspx?i=2661&s=5&c=4

[59] Charlotte Holder Clinger interview with Beth Carmichael, August 8, 2006, Object WV0230.5.001, transcript, Women Veterans Historical Collection, University of North Carolina-Greensboro, Greensboro, NC.
http://library.uncg.edu/dp/wv/results5.aspx?i=2701&s=5&c=4

[60] Dorothy Jane Rechel, interview with Eric Elliott, January 22, 2001, Object WV0196.5.001, transcript, Women Veterans Historical Collection, University of North Carolina-Greensboro, Greensboro, NC.
http://library.uncg.edu/dp/wv/results5.aspx?i=2930&s=5&c=4

[61] Roth, 224.

[62] Fisher, interview.

[63] Rechel, interview.

[64] Appy, 121.

[65] Ibid., 124.

[66] Roth 225; and Offut, 257.

[67] Allen, 242.

[68] Appy, 128.

[69] Rechel, interview.

[70] Roth, 225, 229.

[71] Morden, 247.

[72] Morden, 244.

[73] Ibid., 245. The understanding was that the WACs would *not* be assigned to field installations, and thus would not need the training.

[74] Ibid., 253.

[75] Roth, 226.

[76] Ibid., 226.

[77] Ibid., 225-6.

[78] Ibid.

[79] Morden, 252.

[80] Roth, 230.

[81] Offut, 262.

[82] Jurgevich, 235.

[83] Appy, 144.

[84] Ibid.

[85] Allen, 248-9.

[86] Offut, 261.

[87] Ibuid., 257.

[88] Fisher, interview.

[89] Appy, 239.

[90] Morden, 250.

[91] Jurgevich, 234.

[92] Roth, 231.

[93] Mithers, 81

[94] Morden, 262.

[95] Jurgevich, 238.

[96] Roth, 227;Offut, 259.

[97] Morden, 255.

[98] Gutwillig, 47.

[99] Goldman, 902.

[100] Jeffries-Jones, 145, 151.

[101] Jeffries-Jones, 148.

[102] Estelle B. Freedman, *No Turning back: The History of Feminism and the Future of Women* (New York, Ballantine Books, 2002) 329-30.

[103] Ellen Carol DuBois and Lynn Dumenil, *Through Women's Eyes: An American history with Documents* (New York: Bedford/St Martin's, 2009), 545-546, 673.

[104] Ruth Rosen, *The World Split Open: How the Modern Women's Movement Changed America* (New york, Penguin Books, 2000,2006) 137-138.

[105] Morden, 257.

[106] Bailey, interview.

[107] Barbara L Shay, "A Time to Recognize that Women are Veterans Too," *New York Times* October 28, 1987, A30.

[108] Georgia Dullea, "Like Men who fought, They tell of Anxiety and Painful Recall," *New York Times* May 23.1981, A1.

[109] Roth, 230.

[110] Offut, 265.

[111] Ibid., 267.

[112] Dullea.

[113] Allen, 247, Offut, 260.

[114] Offut, 258, 260,266.

[115] Dullela.

[116] Offut, 268.

[117] Ibid., 267.

[118] Also, very few of the women kept in touch with friends they made in Vietnam.

[119] Morris Janowitz, "The All-Volunteer Military as a 'Sociopolitical' Problem" in *Social problems,* Vol 22, no 3 Feb 1975, 432.

[120] Ibid., 434.

[121] Ibid., 447. Today, women are about 13.4% of the U.S. Army http://www.army.mil/women/today.html

[122] Morden, 257.

[123] Bailey, interview.

About the Author

Amanda R Oviatt served in the US Army from 1998-2002 as a member of the Signal Corps. She served in Darmstadt, Germany at Ft. Bliss Texas. Her interest in women's history really developed during her time as a college student, and this short piece is her personal dedication to the women who served in the military before her.

She currently works at Desert Sea Design, a veteran-owned web design company in Phoenix, Arizona.

She is also the author of *My Lady Olives,* a book about a modern-day Athena and *A Step-by-Step Visual guide to Woo Commerce.*